"BUT THE PENSION FUND WAS JUST SITTING THERE"

And it seemed like such a pittance for Uncle Duke (now general manager of the Washington Redskins) to pay to bring the capital's much-maligned football team back to the top of the NFL standings. Besides, once the rest of the team meets the new recruit, 390-pound "Lava-Lava" Lenny, they aren't going to object too strongly. Meanwhile, Jimmy Carter leafs through the Pentagon's newest weaponry catalogue (he may be able to get a closeout deal on a B-1 bomber), Rick Redfern gets a biorhythm lesson, "Marvelous" Mark Slackmeyer interviews the author of *Mellow: How to Get It*, and Freddy Silverman "exposes" his new plan to boost NBC's ratings. It's all part of the hilarious (and amazingly accurate) world of DOONESBURY.

DOONESBURY

The remarkable comic strip called *Doonesbury* has provoked more public and media reaction than any cartoon in the last twenty-five years, winning legions of loyal followers. Michael J. Doonesbury and the denizens of the Walden Commune appear in nearly four hundred newspapers with a readership of over 23 million.

Bantam Books by G. B. Trudeau
Ask your bookseller for the books you have missed

"But the Pension Fund Was Just Sitting There"

a *Doonesbury* book
by G. B. Trudeau

BANTAM BOOKS
TORONTO • NEW YORK • LONDON

"BUT THE PENSION FUND WAS JUST SITTING THERE"
*A Bantam Book / published by arrangement with
Holt, Rinehart and Winston*

PRINTING HISTORY

*Holt, Rinehart and Winston edition published April 1979
Three printings through September 1979*

*The cartoons in this book appeared in
newspapers in the United States and abroad under
the auspices of Universal Press Syndicate.*

Bantam edition / May 1980

*Bantam Books are published by Bantam Books, Inc.
Its trademark, consisting of the words "Bantam
Books" and the portrayal of a bantam, is Registered
in U.S. Patent and Trademark Office and in other
countries. Marca Registrada. Bantam Books, Inc.,
666 Fifth Avenue, New York, New York 10019.*

PRINTED IN THE UNITED STATES OF AMERICA

0 9 8 7 6 5 4 3 2 1

GOOD EVENING. THIS IS THE SCENE IN NEW YORK TONIGHT AS HUNDREDS OF DEMONSTRATORS GATHER OUTSIDE A DINNER FOR THE EMPRESS OF IRAN. ROLAND HEDLEY IS THERE.

HARRY, THERE'S BEEN A SLIGHT DELAY IN THE FESTIVITIES TONIGHT AS WE AWAIT THE LATE ARRIVAL OF PRO-SHAH FORCES HERE AT THE NEW YORK HILTON HOTEL.

BAD WEATHER APPARENTLY DELAYED THE BUSES BRINGING THE SHAH'S RECRUITS TO N.Y., SO OUT OF FAIRNESS, PLANNERS HAVE HELD UP THE BANQUET TO ALLOW COUNTERDEMONSTRATORS TIME TO TAKE UP THEIR POSITIONS!

...AND HERE THEY COME NOW! LOOKS LIKE THE EVENING'S UNDER WAY, HARRY!

LONG LIVE THE SHAH!

WITH THE SERVING OF A PÂTÉ DE FOIE GRAS AND A LIGHT CHABLIS, THE FRIENDS OF EXXON SOCIETY DINNER HONORING THE SHAHBANOU FARAH IS FINALLY UNDER WAY, HARRY..

DESPITE THE UGLY PROTESTS OUTSIDE, SOME OF OUR BRIGHTEST STARS HAVE TURNED OUT, RANGING FROM VACATIONING NEWSMAN WALTER CRONKITE TO TONIGHT'S BIGGEST SURPRISE, ACTIVIST SHIRLEY MacLAINE!

THE SHAH IS A *MURDERER!* THE SHAH IS A *MUR-DERER!!*

THE SHAH IS.. AWK!

WELL, THE SPEECHES HAVE ALREADY BEGUN HERE AT THE HILTON BALLROOM, HARRY..

THE SHAH IS A MUR-DERER!

HARRY, THE SITUATION HERE ON THE BALLROOM FLOOR IS BEGIN-NING TO HEAT UP, TO SAY THE LEAST.

EVEN AS I SPEAK, ONE TUX-EDOED GENTLEMAN SHOUTING "THE SHAH IS A MURDERER" IS BEING WRESTLED TO THE GROUND BY FOUR DECORUM-MINDED IRANIAN SECURITY AGENTS.

= SCUFFLE! =
= SCUFFLE! =

PRESUMABLY TO STIFLE HIS OUT-BURSTS, A NAPKIN IS NOW BEING STUFFED IN THE MAN'S MOUTH, AN UNNECESSARY MEASURE IN THIS REPORTER'S JUDGMENT, AS A NASTY RABBIT PUNCH HAS ALREADY TAKEN AWAY HIS WIND!

DEMI-TASSE, SIR?

FOR THE EMPRESS'S REACTION, UP TO YOU AT THE HEAD TABLE, BARBARA!

G.B.Trudeau

HEY, DUKE, THERE'S SOME ATTORNEY ON THE PHONE FOR YOU! AN EDWARDS WILLIAMS..

NEVER HEARD OF HIM! I'M NOT HOME!

HE SAYS HE'S WITH THE WASH-INGTON REDSKINS!

OH, *THAT* WILLIAMS! HOT DAMN! HE MUST HAVE GOTTEN MY JOB APPLI-CATION!

WHAT JOB APPLI-CATION?

FOR GENERAL MANAGER! I FINALLY DECIDED IT WAS TIME TO CASH IN ON MY BACKGROUND IN SPORTS MED-ICINE!

YOUR WHAT?

NEPHEW, DID YOU KNOW THREE OUT OF FOUR NFL LINEBACKERS REGULARLY USE AMPHETAMINES?

MR. DUKE, I THINK YOU'RE QUITE MISTAKEN ABOUT THE EXTENT OF THE PILL PROBLEM. WHY, NFL OFFICIALS GIVE ANTI-DRUG LECTURES EVERY MONTH..

YEAH, AND 90% OF YOUR PLAYERS ARE LAUGHING THEIR JOCKS OFF THE WHOLE TIME!

MR. WILLIAMS, YOUR PLAYERS AREN'T PILLHEADS BECAUSE THEY **WANT** TO BE. HELL, NOBODY **LIKES** TAKING PILLS! THEY TAKE 'EM BECAUSE THEY'RE CONCERNED ABOUT WHAT THE NEXT ATHLETE MIGHT BE DOING!

OH.. OH, I SEE.

IT'S A REAL PROBLEM, SIR! AND I'LL TELL YOU, SOMETIMES IT JUST BREAKS MY HEART TO SEE IT!

BUT YOU SAY YOU'VE HAD SOME EXPERIENCE IN THIS AREA?

I'VE BEEN AROUND THE TRACK A FEW TIMES, YES.

GBTrudeau

"...AND WE IN THE FRONT OFFICE OFFER MR. DUKE OUR WARMEST WELCOME TO THE REDSKINS ORGANIZATION!"..OKAY, WE'LL TAKE QUESTIONS NOW..

MR. DUKE, AS FAR AS WE CAN TELL, YOU BRING NO RELEVANT EXPERIENCE TO YOUR JOB. COULD YOU COMMENT?

YEAH. THAT'S A COMPLETE BUNCH OF GARBAGE.

BESIDES MY RECORD IN ADMINISTRATION, I BRING TO MY JOB AN AWESOME EXPERTISE IN SPORTS MEDICINE. IT WILL BE MY DUTY TO SEE THAT EACH AND EVERY MAN IS SAFELY WIRED BEFORE HE GOES OUT ON THAT BALL FIELD!

WHAT? YOU MEAN YOU'LL ACTUALLY BE DISPENSING PILLS?

YES. MY CONTRACT EXPLICITLY..

THANKS FOR COMING, BOYS!

© B Trudeau

..AND THEN THE CAMERA CUTS BACK TO ME ON A MEDIUM CLOSE-UP AS I SAY, "WAS THE CARTER JOURNEY A SUCCESS? ONLY TIME WILL TELL!"

HERE I DROP MY VOICE..."BUT IF THERE WAS ANYTHING OF SUBSTANCE TO BE DIVINED FROM THIS TRIP, IT COMPLETELY ESCAPED THE ATTENTION OF THIS REPORTER!"

THAT'S IT?

YUP. WHAT DO YOU THINK?

SURE YOU CAN AFFORD TO BE THAT HONEST?

HELL, YES! I CALL 'EM AS I SEE 'EM, RICK!

DAN, I THINK THE QUESTION THAT MANY PEOPLE MIGHT HAVE FOR YOU NOW IS, "WHAT WITH ALL THE CUISINARTS, TENNIS LESSONS AND TR-4'S, CAN I REALLY *AFFORD* MELLOW?"

I HEAR YOU, MARK. ONE OF THE MOST COMMON MISCONCEPTIONS ABOUT MELLOW TODAY IS THAT YOU HAVE TO BE UPWARDLY MOBILE, ECONOMICWISE, BEFORE YOU CAN FLASH ON IT!

WELL, IT JUST ISN'T SO! IN FACT, THE EXTENSIVE RESEARCH I DID DURING MY FELLOWSHIP AT THE CALIFORNIA INSTITUTE FOR THE MELLOW STRONGLY SUGGESTS OTHERWISE!

FELLOWSHIP? YOU WERE A MELLOW FELLOW?

IT'S ALL IN MY CHAPTER, "MELLOW ON A FIXED INCOME."

WHAT IS IT, BEV?

MR. DUKE, "LAVA-LAVA" LENNY'S ATTORNEY IS ON THE LINE.

THANKS, BABE. PUT HIM ON.. HELLO, HOOK? IT'S DUKE!

HI, THERE, DUKE! YOU GET MY CONTRACT PROPOSAL YET?

YEAH, I WAS JUST GOING OVER IT, AND IT'S **COMPLETELY** OUT OF LINE! WHAT'S THIS ABOUT THE KID NEEDING HIS OWN UNIVERSAL GYM?

NO CHOICE ON THAT, DUKE. HE'S JUST TOO BIG FOR THE STANDARD MODELS.

OH, YEAH? WELL, HOW ABOUT HIS OWN MEAT LOCKER?

HE'S A GROWING BOY, DUKE! LOOK, YOU WANT A COMPETITOR OR NOT?

WILL THERE BE ANYTHING ELSE, SIR?

YES, DON'T BOTHER TO SEND MR. WIL- LIAMS A COPY OF THE CONTRACT. I'D RATHER EX- PLAIN IT TO HIM IN PERSON..

OH, AND KEEP AN EYE PEELED FOR "LAVA-LAVA" LENNY. HE'S DUE IN FROM THE AIRPORT ANY MINUTE.

YES, SIR. I'LL BUZZ YOU WHEN.. OH, MY GOD!

AH! RIGHT ON TIME!

LET ME SET IT UP FOR YOU, CAMPERS. AS YOU KNOW, I'M FOREGOING THE BOOKS THIS TERM SO I CAN FIND OUT WHETHER BROADCASTING IS THE LIFE FOR ME!

MY FATHER, WHO'S WITH ME HERE IN THE STUDIO TODAY, THINKS I'M WASTING **MY** TIME AND **HIS** MONEY. WHAT DO **YOU** THINK? LET US KNOW. WE'RE TAKING CALLS AT 331-9100!

RING!

?

HELLO? IS THIS MARK'S DAD?

YES, IT IS.

SIT ON IT, MISTER! >GIGGLE!<

I SEE. YOU MUST BE ONE OF MY SON'S LITTLE FANS.

G B Trudeau

YES, AS THE COUNT-DOWN CONTINUES, THE NAME OF THE GAME AT NBC IS "WAITING FOR FREDDY."

CAN SILVERMAN TURN THINGS AROUND FOR THE LOWLY NETWORK? WELL, IT'S ANYONE'S GUESS. IN THE RATINGS GAME THERE IS ONLY ONE QUESTION: HOW LOW ARE YOU WILL-ING TO SINK?

NO ONE, IT SEEMS, IS IMMUNE. EVEN THE NEW TAG-TEAM ANCHOR FORMAT RIGHT HERE AT ABC WIDE WORLD OF NEWS WAS A-DOPTED AS A DESPERATE, LAST-DITCH RESPONSE TO SAGGING RATINGS.

BACK TO YOU, FRANK, PETER, AND MAX.

THANKS.

THANK YOU, ROLLIE.

YES, THANKS. IN OTHER NEWS..

THE LONG VIGIL IS OVER. EVEN AS I SPEAK, FRED P. SILVERMAN IS SPINNING HIS MILLION-DOLLAR WHEELS FOR THIRD-PLACE NBC!

ALREADY, THE NEW MAN HAS BEGUN TO LIVE UP TO HIS IMAGE AS A HARD WORKER. SILVERMAN IS SAID TO HAVE REPORTED TO WORK THIS MORNING AT 5:30 A.M.!

AND NOW, AMIDST GROWING RUMORS THAT THEIR NEW BOSS EVEN SKIPPED LUNCH, NBC EXECUTIVES ARE ANXIOUSLY AWAITING THE OUTCOME OF FREDDY'S PROGRAMING MAGIC!

ANY CHANGE YET?

YES..YES! BY GOD, HE'S TURNING IT AROUND!

LOOK OUT, WONDER CHIMP!

BLAM! BLAM!

GOOD NEWS, BOYS AND GIRLS! THIS IS ZONKER HARRIS, SUBBING FOR "MARVELOUS" MARK SLACKMEYER!

HOW COME? WELL, MARK'S ON HIS WAY TO WASHINGTON, D.C., TO TALK TO REPRESENTATIVE LACEY DAVENPORT ABOUT THE KOREAN SCANDAL! HOT STUFF, HUH?

WBBY WILL BE BROADCASTING THAT INTERVIEW LIVE. SO IF YOU'VE GOT ANY QUESTIONS FOR THE CONGRESSWOMAN, JUST PHONE 'EM IN!

RINGG!

TALK TO ME!

WHAT KOREAN SCANDAL? I'VE BEEN OUT OF TOWN.

HI, THIS IS MARK SLACK- MEYER, AND I'M TALKING TO HOUSE ETHICS COMMIT- TEE STALWART, CONGRESS- WOMAN LACEY DAVENPORT.

MRS. DAVENPORT, AFTER 20 MONTHS OF INQUIRY, YOUR INVESTIGATION HAS PRODUCED EVIDENCE THAT SOME 35 MEMBERS OF CONGRESS TOOK MONEY FROM A KOREAN AGENT. AND YET NO DISCIPLINARY ACTION OF **ANY** KIND HAS BEEN INITIATED!

WOULDN'T YOU SAY THAT THE COMMIT- TEE'S FAILURE TO ACT CONSTITUTES AN ENDORSEMENT OF CORRUPTION AMONG ITS OWN?

I COULDN'T AGREE MORE, DEAR BOY. WOULD YOU CARE FOR SOME MORE TEA?

UH..NO, THANK YOU. I'M IN THE MIDDLE OF AN INTERVIEW.

WHY, YES, OF COURSE, YOU ARE. GO RIGHT AHEAD, DEAR.